IN THE LIGHT OF

CIARAN CARSON

IN THE LIGHT OF

after *illuminations* by arthur rimbaud

Wake Forest University Press

First North American edition

ISBN 978-1-930630-62-8

Library of Congress
Catalog Number: 2012954305

Wake Forest University Press
WWW.WFU.EDU/WFUPRESS
Post Office Box 7333
Winston-Salem, NC 27109

Contents

for Colin Graham

Author's Note

I

There are many enigmas surrounding the life and work of Arthur Rimbaud (1854-1891), not least in the matter of the background, origin and composition of the *Illuminations*, a possibly unfinished collection of forty prose poems and two in free verse. The manuscripts, so far as we know, are undated, without any indication as to how the poems should be ordered; but it is generally thought that they were written sporadically between 1872 and 1875, in various locations, including Paris, London and Belgium, and that some of them may (or may not) constitute Rimbaud's last poetic work. What we do know is that the manuscripts were once in the possession of Rimbaud's erstwhile lover, the poet Paul Verlaine, and that the majority of the poems were first published in 1886 by the Symbolist review *La Vogue*, which referred to their author as 'the late Arthur Rimbaud' and 'the equivocal and glorious deceased'. It seems Verlaine had written to Rimbaud, then in Africa; receiving no reply, he assumed he was dead. Later in 1886 *La Vogue* published the *Illuminations* in volume form, with a preface by Verlaine in which he explained: '*Le mot* Illuminations *est anglais et veut dire gravures colorées* — coloured plates', though it is unclear whether Rimbaud himself chose the title. If he did, it might conform to his eccentric or playful use of 'English' titles for the poems 'Being Beauteous' and 'Bottom', for 'Illuminations' is not, as Verlaine states, an English word meaning 'coloured plates'.

The only definition for 'illumination' in the Oxford English Dictionary which resembles Verlaine's is 'formerly, also, the colouring of maps or prints', as in '1678 E. Phillips *New World of Words* (ed 4), a laying of colours upon Maps or Printed Pictures; so as to give the greater light, as it were, and beauty to them'. This is not quite 'illumination' in the English sense of decorating letters in a text (*enluminure* in French), which might lie at the back of Verlaine's 'coloured plates'; but illuminations can also be a show of festive lights, or, appropriately for Rimbaud, divine or poetic inspiration. In his famous '*lettre du voyant*', Rimbaud declared: 'One must, I say, be a seer, make oneself a seer. The poet makes himself a seer through a long, prodigious and rational disordering of all the senses.' However we gloss the title *Illuminations*, the poems flit within the inward eye like brightly-coloured magic lantern slides, pictures from a marvellous book, visions of another world, scenes from an avant-garde film. Rimbaud was avant-garde before the Avant-garde; a surrealist before Surrealism; and, environmentalist *avant la lettre*, his critique of industrial society in some of these poems is still relevant today. In all those senses he was indeed a seer.

2

In 1998 I published *The Alexandrine Plan*, translations or adaptations of sonnets by Rimbaud, Baudelaire and Mallarmé. My concern in that book was not so much to give a 'literal' meaning of what the poems might be saying, as to reproduce the original metre in English, and see what interpretations might emerge from those constraints, both of rhyme and the twelve syllables of the classical French alexandrine. Shortly afterwards I thought I might attempt a translation of some of the poems in *Illuminations*; but, try as I might, I could not arrive at any form of words that did justice to the originals, to my understanding of what they might imply or mean, or to my sense of their music. What I did seemed inert, flabby, prosaic, and too close to whatever English translations I had consulted to augment my passable French. I could find no edge to the matter. I retired defeated and forgot about the whole brief affair.

Then, on 3 April 2012 (Shrove Tuesday, as it happened), I received an email from Colin Graham of the National University of Ireland, Maynooth, asking if I might be interested in doing versions of seven of the prose poems from *Illuminations*, which would then be worked on by graphic designers for an exhibition in the new 'Illuminations' gallery at Maynooth. I had not done any kind of poetry for some time, and the invitation seemed serendipitous. On Spy Wednesday I had a kind of illumination of my own: rather than translate the prose poems as prose poems, I could perhaps adapt them to an Alexandrine format of twelve-syllable rhyming couplets — Rimbaud crossed with Racine, as it were. I set to the next day, Holy Thursday, and somehow within a week I had arrived at twenty-two such versions. I spent the next few weeks tweaking and tinkering, and added three prose versions to frame what had now become a book: not the book that is Rimbaud's *Illuminations*, but another, taken from that book.

At first, it seemed perverse to translate prose poems into verse: but the more I worked the more it became apparent that many passages in Rimbaud's musical prose could be read as verse, with a prosody of their own, scanned, rhymed, alliterated. One could see incipient sonnets embedded therein; and it happened that several of my versions came out as fourteen lines. So I began to think of the project as a restoration, or renovation, rather than a complete makeover. In any event these versions are not conventional translations. The constraints of rhyme and metre led me to cut, interpolate, and interpret. There are instances where I have added to or taken away from the original. I have sometimes twisted Rimbaud's words. And Rimbaud's words, of course, twisted mine. Examining his French, I had also to examine my English, learning other aspects of it, sometimes relearning it, for one can never fully know a language, which is always bigger than any of us. As Walter Benjamin has it in 'The Task of the Translator' (one of a number of essays collected under the English title *Illuminations*), '[The translator] must expand and deepen his language by means of the foreign language.' One's 'own' language begins to seem another.

So in translation one necessarily becomes Another. First-person, third-person, noun and verb, become confused: *Je est un autre*, 'I is another', as Rimbaud has it. I began by wanting to obey the constraints of the twelve syllables of the alexandrine, but that proved impossible: the line, under the pressure of Rimbaud's sometimes elaborate and often elliptical syntax, began to lengthen or contract in places, and thus became even more hybrid than what I had envisaged. I was not too put out by this failure to abide by my own rule: the prose poems seemed to want that variation of pace and rhythm; written in different voices, different keys as it were, they vary considerably in their linguistic strategies. The strain of the verse form grafted on to Rimbaud's prose led to hybrid: translation as mutation. Having said all that, I have 'translated' as closely to my understanding of the original as I could, when I could. The result of my deliberations follows. Or rather, it has gone before, since this Author's Note, like all such introductions, has been written after the event.

intro

Vigil (from Veillées*)*

Once more the lighting returns to the central beam, the roof-tree. From the two far ends of the room — nondescript stage sets — harmonic elevations merge or mingle. The wall facing the spectator is a '*succession psychologique*' of cross sections, friezes, atmospheric bands and geological happenstance. Intense and rapid dream of sentimental groups of beings, of every possible character, under every possible appearance.

act one

As I Roved Out (Aube)

I embraced the summer dawn. All was still before
the palaces, their waters dead forevermore.

Shade after shadow lingered on the woodland road.
I woke quick, live, warm clouds of breath as on I strode.

Gemstones eyed my passing. Wings arose without sound.
My first adventure happened on a path I found

already littered with pale glints, wherein a flower
spoke her name to me. I blinked. It was no known hour.

I laughed to see the Wasserfall dishevelling itself
in shocks among the pines; climbing shelf by rocky shelf,

I recognized the goddess at the silvered peak.
Voilà! Veil after veil I lifted from her, not to speak

of how my arms were fluttering as I did so.
I did it in the lane. And boldly did I go

across the plain where I betrayed her to the cock.
She fled to the city under the steeple clock,

and beggar-like I tailed her on the marble quays.
Far up the road, beneath a grove of laurel trees,

I wound her in those recollected veils, and realized,
just a little, something of her massive shape and size.

Then dawn and child, finding themselves in the wood,
sank deep down into it. On waking it was noon.

After Me . . . (Après le Déluge)

Once the notion of 'The Flood' had dwindled away
a hare halted in sweet hay where the harebells sway

and said its prayer to the rainbow through a spider's web.
And oh! the precious stones were hiding, or had ebbed,

what flowers there were already pivoting to look.
A dirty main street: stalls being set up, boats hauled crook

by hook towards the sea, delineated wave on wave
as in an old engraving. Blood flowed in the nave

of Bluebeard's Castle, from dark slaughterhouses flowed,
every window blanched by God's Seal. Blood and milk flowed.

Beavers busied themselves building. Tall tasses steamed
in coffee houses. In the mansion, rain still streamed

down the windows, children dressed in mourning black
gazed at engaging images. A door clacked;

and in the village square a child whirled his arms about,
understood by weathervane, steeple-cock and rainspout.

Madame Blank established a piano in the Alps.
A thousand First Communion Masses packed the apse.

Caravans embarked. L'Hôtel Splendide was built
on icy chaos, polar night and snowy milt.

Ever afterward, the Moon heard jackals cackling
in the Wastes of Thyme, and eclogues of clogs clacking

in the orchard. Then in the fluorescing violet
forest, the fair nymph Eucharis revealed that it

was spring. Pond, overflow! Foam, overwhelm the bridge,
and slather through the woods! Lightning and thunder, rage!

Black draperies and church organs, rise and roll through rain,
and summon up the former Deluge once again!

For since it has evaporated — oh, the precious stones
being buried, and the flowers fully blown! —

it's such a bore! And the Queen, the Witch, the Sorceress
who fans her embers in an earthen crock, will ne'er confess,

nor tell that which she's always known,
which is that which we'll never know.

Snow (Fleurs)

From a golden staircase — among the silken cords
on gauze of grey, plush velvets lush as greensward,

discs of crystal blackening like bronze when struck
by noon — I see the foxglove open on a ruck

of carpet wrought with silver filigree of eyes
and tresses. Pieces of yellow gold strewn slantwise

over agate, tall piers of pernambuco wood
supporting domes of emerald in the interlude

of bouquets of white satin sporting on ruby sprays,
surround the water-rose's delicate display.

And like a god with huge blue eyes and arms of snow
the sea and sky pull towards the marble terraces

great crowds of white roses rising in crescendo
as forever young forever strong they grow and grow.

Cities (Villes)

Some cities, for whose populations are revealed
these Alleghenies and these Lebanons of dream!

See how the chalets built of wood and crystal move
along on blind pulleys and invisible grooves.

Copper palm trees, and colossuses, surround
the ancient craters from which Vulcan tunes resound.

The Festival of Bawd rings out above the red
canals which hang behind the chalets overhead.

Carillons in full cry tumble down the gorges.
Guilds of giant choristers rush through, gorgeous

in their oriflammes and vestments dazzling with the light
that falls upon the mountain peaks of celestite.

From platforms among precipices Rolands blare
their trumpets of bravura through the limpid air.

On hotel roofs and gangways over the abyss
heat-waves shimmer banners of aurora borealis.

The lapsed apotheoses join the Alpine fields
where seraph centauresses wander unconcealed

among the avalanches. On a level way
above the highest peak, a great sea troubled by

th'eternal birth of Venus, packed with Orpheonic craft
and bubbly pearls and babbling conches fore and aft,

the waters darkening sporadically with deadly blows.
Bunches of flowers thick as guns or goblets bellow below.

Trains of Mabs in opaline and russet dresses
climb the steep ravines where fall the silver tresses

of a waterfall and stags with brambly antlers sit
up to their hocks in it to suckle at Diana's tit.

Bacchantes of the suburbs sob their Bacchic song,
the moon responds with lightning shocks and howls along.

Venus appears in the ironmaster's forge.
Sheaves of campaniles blow forth music from the core:

music of the peoples. From castles built of bone
come undreamed-of melodies hitherto unknown.

All the legends break loose as moose throughout the streets.
The paradise of storm subsides into defeat.

Savage ceaseless beings dance the Festival of Dark.
And once upon a time I flew down happy as a lark

into a bustling Baghdad boulevard, where throngs
gave out the joy of fresh-discovered work in song

against a thickly woven breeze, and they were powerless
to elude the fabled phantoms of Parnassus

where they were destined to have met. What helping hand,
what happy hour will give me back that Otherland

whence come all my slumbers and my dreams,
my stirrings howsoever slight, and everything is what it seems?

Seer (Mystique)

On the slant of a slope, angels wheel their robes of wool
and spin in ceremony on fields of emerald and steel.

Flames leap from the meadow grasses to the top
of the hill-breast. To the left, the leaf-mould's been cropped

by war horses, trodden by homicides. Pandemonium
their parabola. Behind the right-hand ridge, the datum

line of Orients and progress. And while the band
at the top of the scene is a frieze of the sea meeting sand —

swashing of conches, the chatter of glasses in bars —
the night sky blossoming with aromatic stars,

and more, moreover, sways like a basket let down
opposite the slope, against our face, and we drown
in the blue abyss blossoming below the town.

Poles Apart (Métropolitain)

From the Ossianic Ocean to the Straits of Indigo,
on rose and orange sands washed by the Sky of Vino,

crystal boulevards have sprung up, newly occupied by
poor families who make do from market stalls: The City.

Tumbling from the Wastes of Bitumen down the slippery slopes
where coils of horrible fog stretch out in monstrous ropes

across the sky that billows, rolls, descends, recedes, in all
the sinister black smoke the oceanic pall

can body forth, are helmets, cartwheels, bobbing bottles,
scuttled submarines and horses' rumps: The Battle.

Lift your head: that arched wooden bridge; those last
market gardens of Samaria; those masks whipped by the blast

and reddened by the lantern on a freezing night;
that girl gone down the river in her gaudy dress, a water-sprite;

those luminous skulls among the rows of peas,
and all the other mad phantasmagoria: The Rural Scene.

Those roads bordered by railings and walls that barely contain
their budding groves, and frightful flowers you might name

'Love' and 'Dove', damask roses languishing in boredom,
properties of faery aristocracies, and foreign kingdoms,

still receivers of the ancient music howsoever.
And there are inns already that are closed forever.

There are princesses; and if by now you're not completely high,
there's the study of the stars: The Sky.

That morning when, with Her, you struggled under those blows
of snow, those green lips, those blocks of ice, those

black banners, and blue beams of gleaming lunar length,
those purple perfumes of the polar sun: Your Strength.

Phases of the Moon (Phrases)

1

When the world has dwindled to a single dark wood
gawped at by these four kindred eyes — to where we stood

on a beach, two loyal children — to the musical house
we loved to delve in — I'll find you, little mouse.

Should there be but one solitary old man, calm
and bearded in his luxury — I'll kneel before you, little ma'am.

Should I realize every one of your memories,
should I be she who knows the muzzle — I'll suffocate you,
little tease.

2

When we are strong as strong, who backs down? When gay
as gay,
who falls about with laughter? When nasty, nasty, what can
they say?

Put on your finery, and dance, and laugh. Reap and sow.
I never could throw love out the window.

3

Beggar-girl, monstrous child, my counterpart! It's all the same
to you, these miserable women on the game,

their wiles my quandary. O wrap me to you with that voice
of yours, impossible voice! That flatters my despair, my vice.

4

Overcast morning in July. A taste of ashes
drifts through the sweaty air. A smell of wood sleazes

on the hearth. Fetid flowers. Chaos on the boulevards,
canal mist dank on the fields. Why not incense and peignoirs?

5

I have stretched ropes from steeple to steeple, garlands
from window to window; gold chains from star to star, and
  I dance.

6

The mountain pool smokes night and day.
What witch will loom against the pallid sunset? What spray
of violets fall into the white décolleté?

7

While public funds are squandered by the great and good and
  proud,
a bell of rose-coloured fire tolls in the clouds.

8

Reviving a pleasant taste of India ink, a black
powder drizzles on my vigil. I consult the almanac,

turn down the gaslight, throw myself onto the bed.
And, turning towards the shadows of a riverbed,

I see you, O my lovely girls, my queens, emerge
in dripping radiance to drag me from the verge!

Fée (Fairy)

All for Helen, ornamental oozing saps collogued
in virgin shadows: silent, unmoved, glittering the astral road.

Summer's torrid heat was given over to the mute birds,
inevitable languor to an expensive funeral barge

through winding estuaries of loves long dead;
and perfumes like an evanescent freshet overlaid

the chorus of the Timberwomen to the rumble
of the torrent through the ruined wood, from the cowbells

in the valleys echoing the long cries of the steppes;
all for Helen, bushy furs and shadows quivered, bee-skeps

oozed, the poor shivered, shimmering the celestial legends.
And her eyes, her dancing far superior to a thousand

precious dazzles coldly flowing in, or to the pleasure
of that unique décor, that one and only hour.

Demotic Nocturne (Nocturne vulgaire)

A breath cleaves operatic breaches in the walls
of shimmery, dilapidated marble halls,

disperses all the boundaries of hearth and home,
and blurs the casement windows with a faery foam.

One foot planted on a gargoyle, shimmying along
the grapevine, I fell into this coach whose chaise longue

interior bespoke antique, as did the panes
of bull's-eye glass, the panels boasting marbled veins.

Hearse of my sleep, my bucolic folly caravan veers on
the verge of the overgrown high road to Bygone.

And swirling in a window-bubble north-north-west
I saw pale lunar figures, leaves, and breasts.

Deep bottle blue and verdigris invade the scene,
unhitch the horses teetering along the scree.

This is where you whistle up the storm of Sodom,
vicious beasts, and armies wreaking drunken bedlam.

Postilion and dream animals, will they reprise
themselves below the suffocating forest trees,

to plunge me headlong in the fount of silk? And send
us lashed across these lapping waters I have penned,

across a floor awash with shattered glass and drink
to roll before the barking mastiffs black as ink,

whose jaws dispense a cataract of awful foam . . .
a breath disperses all the boundaries of home.

La Bête (Bottom)

Reality being too prickly for my big personality,
I found myself nonetheless chez Milady,

as a great big grey-blue bird soaring to the ceiling
cornice, trailing my wings through the shades of evening.

I became, at the foot of the four-poster bed
which hid her adorable jewellery, her golden braid,

her physical masterworks, a great big bear
with violet gums, fur grizzled with grief, my eyes on the pair

of silver and crystal consoles. All became shadow
and glowing aquarium. Come morning, I rushed out to go —

brave dawn of June — braying on to the fields,
brandishing my great big donkey grievance, till the well-heeled

Sabine suburban housewives from beyond the railway track
flew madly to throw themselves on my donkey-rough neck.

Lives (Vies)

1

O the enormous avenues of the Holy Land,
the terraces of the Temple! The desert sand!

What has become of him, the Brahman who explained
the Book of Proverbs to me as if preordained?

And even the old women of that time and place,
I see them still! And I remember azure space,

the silver hours and sunlit rivers, my companion's
hand on my shoulder, as on the peppery plains

we caressed each other. Thundering about my thought,
a flight of scarlet pigeons. Exiled, I had wrought

a stage on which to realize all the masterpieces
of dramatic literature from West to East.

I could show you untold riches. I could tell
tales of treasures found by you. I'd know the sequel.

My wisdom? Scorned as chaos. What's my nothingness
to the wonders that await you, and will leave you speechless?

2

I am an inventor such as never yet was seen;
moreover, a musician of the Hippocrene

who has discovered something like the clef of love.
At present, as a country gentleman, I live

off my meagre lands and modest piece of sky,
trying to rejuvenate the memory

of my beggar childhood, my apprenticeship,
arriving in my clogs, and then the slip on slip

of half a dozen widowhoods, the raucous nights
when, sober-headed as I was, I could not rise

to the occasion of my comrades' capriccioso.
Though I don't regret my divine former ego:

the sober air of this bleak country keeps me well
supplied with scepticism. But since I'm compelled

to say that scepticism doesn't pay the bills,
and I'm devoted to a newer set of ills,

watch out! For very soon now I expect to be
a lunatic of high and dangerous degree!

3

In a loft in which they locked me at the age
of twelve, I came to know the world. I was a page

in *La Comédie Humaine*. In a cellar I learned
History. In a northern city, at a nocturne

revel, the Old Masters' mistresses were brought
to me. In a gloomy Paris arcade I was taught

Astronomy. And in a most superior abode
surrounded by the entire Orient below,

I worked prodigiously until my oeuvre was complete,
then spent my time there in illustrious retreat.

I've brewed my blood. Paid all my dues. I really do come
from beyond the tomb. Commissions? That I've done.

interlude

Tale (Conte)

A prince was not happy with himself because until then he had put all his energies into perfecting vulgar liberalities. He foresaw astounding revolutions of love, and suspected his wives could do better than complaisance ornamented by celestial luxury. He wished to see the truth, the hour of essential desire and satisfaction. Aberration of piety or not, that was what he wished for. He had a tolerable amount of worldly power at his disposal.

All the women who had known him were put to death: what plunder in the Garden of Beauty! Under the sabre's edge, they gave him their blessing. He did not order any new ones. Women reappeared.

He put to death all who followed him on hunting or drinking expeditions. Everyone followed him.

He entertained himself in slitting the throats of rare beasts. He set palaces in flames. He would pounce on his people and hack them to pieces. Still the hoi polloi, the golden roofs, the splendid animals remained.

Can one find bliss through mass destruction, rejuvenation through cruelty? There was not so much as a murmur from the masses. No one ventured an opinion.

One evening he was haughtily galloping. A Genie appeared, a being of ineffable, emphatic beauty. His countenance and bearing displayed the promise of a manifold and complex love! Nay, of inexpressible and unendurable felicity! It is probable that the Prince and the Genie annihilated each other in perfect health. How could they not help but die of it? So they died together.

But the Prince passed away in his palace, at a normal age. The Prince was the Genie. The Genie was the Prince.

Deep music falls short of our desire.

act two

Invisible Cities (Les Ponts)

Skies a crystal grey. Bizarre design of bridges, some straight,
some humpbacked, others looping down oblique and angulate,

a design repeated in the other, lighted circuits
of the grand canal, but all so long and delicate

that the docks, overloaded with domes, are lowered
and diminished. A few of the said bridges are still covered

with hovels. Others support poles, frail parapets and tropes.
Minor chords cross each other and fade away; ropes

ascend from the embankments. You can make out a red coat,
perhaps other costumes; musical instruments you may note.

Are these popular tunes, snatches of seigneurial spree,
fragments of public anthems? Wide as an arm of the sea,

the water is grey and blue. A white ray
falling from the outer sky annihilates this comedy.

On the Road (Enfance)

I

Black-eyed idol, shocked with yellow hair, of no known clan
or ancestry, yet nobler than fable, Mexican

crossed with Flemish; her domain the arrogant azure
and forty shades of greenery which court the shore

called into being by the shipless waves which speak
its place names of barbaric Slavic, Celtic, Greek.

At the brink of the forest — dream flowers tingle, flash
and flare — the girl with orange lips, her knees sashed

by the glassy flood that gushes from the meadows,
body bare but shimmering and clothed by flora, rainbow,

sea and shadow. Ladies stroll on terraces
adjacent to the sea. There are girls and giantesses,

tall black women proud amid the mossy verdigris,
jewels standing in the fat soil of the seaside groves

and thawing flowerbeds. Young mums the images
of big sisters with their eyes full of pilgrimages;

sultanas, swanky princesses in haughty haute couture
and little foreign girls, and girls in melancholic sweet amour.

Quel ennui, the hours of murmuring, '*Ma chérie*,
I know just how you feel . . . He will come round, you'll see.'

2

That's her, the little dead girl, behind the bed of roses.
Mamma, passed away, passes down the steps. To the roses.

Cousin's carriage squeaks on the sand. The sun
sets on little brother (he's in India!) in the red carnation

meadow. And the old men buried, for their part,
bolt upright in the wallflower-covered rampart.

A swarm of golden leaves surrounds the general's house.
You take the red road to the empty inn. We're in the South.

The chateau's up for sale, the shutters hanging loose.
The curate has the keys to the church: it's no longer in use.

Around the park the keepers' cottages lie forlorn,
the fences overgrown with rustling, sky-scraping thorn.

In any case there's nothing to be seen beyond the trees.
The meadows climb to hamlets without anvil or cock.

The sluice gate lies open. O Calvaries
and windmills of the wilderness, the isles of haycock.

3

Magic flowers buzzed. Hill slopes rocked him to and fro.
Fabulously elegant monsters performed a mambo.

Clouds fattening and floating tier upon tier
over the high seas gathered from an eternity of tears.

4

In the woods there is a bird. His song stops you. You blush.
There is a clock that never strikes. You hear the hush.

There is a pothole in which white things seethe around.
There is a lake that goes up, and a steeple that goes down.

There is a little carriage in the copse, abandoned
or it's running away down the road beribboned.

There's a troupe of strolling players and their motley brood
glimpsed on the road through the trees at the edge of the wood.

And then, when you're hungry and thirsty, there's always
somebody to chase you away.

5

I am the saint at prayer on the terrace skyline
like the beasts which graze down to the sea of Palestine.

I am the scholar in the armchair in the dark eyrie.
Rain and branches beat against the casements of the library.

I am the wanderer of the high road through
the blasted dwarfish woods; the roar of sluices

deafens my footsteps. For a long time I sit stunned
by the melancholy gold laundry of the setting sun.

I might well be the child abandoned on the pier
floating out to the high seas, the little muleteer

Following the mountain track which climbs to the sky.
The paths are rough, hillocks spiked with gorse nearby.

How still the air! How far away the springs and birds!
This must be the end of the world. Ever onwards upwards.

6

When the bit comes to the bit, let them rent
me this tomb covered in bumpy whitewashed cement,

deep down in the earth. I lean my elbow on
the desk. I read by lamplight, fool enough to con

these boring books again. Enormously remote
above my subterranean salon, houses send down roots,

fogs gather. The muck is red or black. Monstrous
city, endless night! Not so far above, the noxious

sewers. Their walls the very thickness of the globe.
Chasms of azure, walls of fire? I send a probe

into these levels, maybe to discover this is where
moons encounter comets, and pterodactyls whirr.

In hours of bitterness I imagine spheres of sapphire
and of metal. I am master of silence. I hear no choir.

Why then, for all the cynicism that I vaunt,
should the ghost of a vent pale in the corner of my vault?

What Goes Round (Ornières)

To the right, the summer dawn awakes the leaves,
the mists, the noises of the park, and pales the palings' sheaves.

And the slopes to the left hold in their violet shadows
the thousand quickening ruts of the dewy road.

Fairytale procession! Wagons loaded with animals
of gilded wood, rainbow-hued poles and awnings and panels,

all drawn by twenty galloping dappled circus horses, men
and children bouncing on marvellous animals — twice times ten

vehicles bedecked with flowers, ornate as coaches from a fairy tale,
brimming with children dressed up for a suburban pastoral —

coffins under ebon canopies each swaying their pair
of black plumes to the trot of huge blue and black mares.

Curtain Raiser (Parade)

Most sturdy rogues. Several of them have ripped you off.
Such little needs they have, no rush to take advantage of

you, knowing what they do about you. What mature men!
Eyes blank as the summer night, eyes of energumen,

red and black and tricoloured, steel studded with gold stars;
faces distorted, leaden, pale, aflame. Burlesque bazaar!

Cruel, gaudy swank and swagger. Some are young — how
would they regard Cherubino? — well endowed

with terrifying voices. A bunch of very dangerous clowns,
they're sent to take it up the back way in the nearest town,

dressed to kill. O most brutal leering paradise
of smirk and sneer! Not to be compared with your prize

fakirs or your average buffoon. In furbelows and frills
like something from a bad dream, they dance quadrilles,

play romances, tragedies, villains, demi-gods and queens
in histories or religions that have never been.

Chinese, Hottentots, bohemians and nitwits,
Molochs, lizards of the lounge, hyenas, little squits,

they mix up clapped-out schticks with sleazy poses,
or the latest sketch; sing girly arias on tippy-toes.

Master jugglers, they transpose the fore to aft,
and cunningly deploy electrifying stagecraft.

Eyes blaze, rouge weeps, bones stretch, blood sings.
Whether travesty or terror, they aim to do their thing —

which lasts a minute or whole months on end.
And who's behind this wild curtain raiser? I, my friend.

Cities (Villes)

The official acropolis exceeds the most
colossal modern barbarity, not to boast

of the dull light ever leaching from the grey sky,
the imperial glare of the buildings. Snow lies

all the year round. A singular enormity
of awful taste has reproduced by committee

the architectures of the Ancient World. I go
to shows of paintings whose quality is zero,

in premises the size of twenty Hampton Courts.
'Simply not to be missed', according to reports.

A Norwegian Nebuchadnezzar has constructed
the marble ministerial staircase as instructed;

even the lackeys, prouder than Brahmans, look down
their noses at you, and I tremble at the frown

of the colossal doormen, not to talk of foremen.
And can you find your way around? Ask the taxi-men —

they'll go on all day about closed squares, cul-de-sacs,
security barriers. It fairly puts their backs

up, I can tell you. As for the parks, here you find
'Primitive nature organized by high art'. Mind

you, it's inexplicable, this part of the town:
a boatless arm of the sea shivers its sleet-blue gown

between quays decked out with giant candelabra.
'Ministry of Works': the usual palabra.

A little pontoon leads you to a postern gate
right under the dome of 'Sainte-Chapelle'. It's really great:

diameter of said dome, fifteen thousand feet.
Having said that, parts of it are still incomplete.

The brass footbridges offer certain points of view
from platforms and stairs from which I thought I'd see through

to the depths of the acropolis. Here's the wonder
I could not discover: how a man might wander

on all the other levels above or below
the city. Where might they be found? Which way to go?

For the contemporary visitor, to check
his whereabouts would take at least an all-day trek.

The business district is a circus, uniformly styled,
extensive galleries and arcades undefiled

by shops, though the snow has been trampled on the roadside:
nabobs, rare as London Sunday morning walkers, stride

towards a diamond coach. Several divans of red velvet;
polar drinks are served, at prices variably elevated —

anything from eight hundred to eight thousand
rupees; more, if you happen to come from Iceland.

Are there theatres to be found in this zone of snow?
Maybe the boutiques put on the odd, small, sordid show.

And there must be a police force, though what strange laws
apply here are beyond me. It's given me some pause,

trying to conceive of what adventurers venture here.
It must be said the suburb has an atmosphere

as elegant as a beautiful Paris street. Democrats
are but a hundred strong; the houses are detached:

the suburb peters out bizarrely in the woods of what
they call 'The County'. There are groves abounding in foxtrot,

immense plantations yielding all kinds of delight,
where untamed gentlemen hunt through the journals by night,
scanning for gossip or sport by the newly invented light.

Être Belle (Being beauteous)

Against a snow, a Being Beautiful of great size.
Death-whistles and circles of mute music give rise

to this adorable hulk, and make it get up
spectre-like to loom and quiver. Seen in close-up,

wounds of black and scarlet burst through the haughty flesh.
The colours of real life shimmer, flit and flash

about this apparition in the builder's yard.
Shudders grumble thunder as — electric-charged

with spits and blips of deadly static that the world,
receding ever further like a marble swirled

in space behind us, hurls against our Mother
of Beauty — she backs off, straightens, and becomes another.

And oh! our bones are clothed anew with flesh and sex.
O ashen face, O hair escutcheon, what comes next?

The cannon against which I am saboteur
amid the clash of trees and weightless air.

The Twilight of History (Soir historique)

In whatever evening the naïve tourist happens
to be, escaping from our economic horrors,

a master's hand awakes the spinet of the meadows.
They're playing cards in the depths of the pond; posed

in the mirror are cuties and queens; there are female
saints, veils, threads of harmony, legendary scales

of colour iridescent in the setting sun.
He shudders as hunt and horde rush by. A gun

sounds. Hullaballoo. Drama drips on the stage of grass.
Watch the ceiling people bang their heads against the glass!

To his captive vision, Germany scaffolds upwards
to the moon; Tatar deserts catch fire; blizzard

revolutions sweep Celestial China; detailed
by stairs and armchairs cut into the rock, a little world, pale

and flat — Africa the Occident — will come to pass.
Afterwards, the ballet of familiar seas and nights, worthless

chemistry and empty arias. The same small-town
bourgeois magic wherever the mail boat sets you down.

Even the most elementary physicist feels
it's impossible to endure this egotistical zeal,

the mist of physical regret, which even to observe
is more than any sane tellurian deserves.

No! The moment of the boiler room, of rising seas,
of subterranean stirrings, of the planet seized

by conflagration, and the consequent exterminations,
certainties so blithely skimmed by Biblical interpretation,

by the Norms . . . we need serious people to see through it.
Though that's hardly the stuff of legend, I admit.

The Point (Promontoire)

Golden dawn and shivering evening find our ship
riding just off this villa and its dependent townships

which comprise a promontory extensive as Epirus
or Greater Japan, Arabia and the Peloponnesus!

Shrines illuminated by returning embassies;
vast panoramas of the coastal cheveaux-de-frise;

dunes illustrious with sultry flowers and bacchanals;
levees of a sleazy Venice, and Carthaginian canals;

drowsy eruptions of Etnas, flowers and water in crevasses;
glaciers; wash-houses surrounded by German aspens;

slopes of magnificent parks; circular façades
of Grand Hotels in Brooklyn; while their railways, I should add,

go under, round, and overhang the premises,
selected from historical examples of naves and apses

from the most colossal architectural gazebos
culled from Asia, the Americas and Italy, whose windows,

lit by champagne, chandeliers and heady breezes, open
to the whim of travellers and nobles, welcome in

through daylight hours a host of coastal ritornellos,
not to mention the most artistic tarentellas,
all to decorate the grand façades of Promontory Palace.

High Society (Scènes)

The Ancient Theatre persues its musical accords
and divides its idylls: boulevards of trestle boards.

A wooden pier extends the length of a stony field
where the uncouth wander under the naked trees.

In corridors of black gauze designed by troglodytes,
pursuing the promenaders under lantern-light

and leaves, bird actors swoop onto a pontoon
of masonry hitched to a flotilla of balloons

pitching and yawing amid the archipelago
of crowded jolly boats and pleasure-cruising bateaux.

Lyric scenes accompanied by drum and flute
look down from niches intricate and convolute

contrived upon the ceilings of a modern club
or hall of Orient, or renovated pub.

The Faery Spectacle manoeuvres on a summit
of the amphitheatre in a wooden thicket,

or sings and shimmies for the ignorami
in the shadow of the waving forest's origami

which overhangs the ridge of cultivated fields.
On this our stage, the Opéra-Comique can be seen
between the gallery and footlights. What a scene.

Antic (Antique)

Elegant son of Pan! About your forehead crowned
with wild flowerets and berries, you move around

those precious orbs, your eyes. Stained with brown lees
of wine, your cheeks grow hollow. Your fangs gleam.

Your chest is a lyre, plucked strings shivering the blond hair
of your arms. Your heart pulses in the dark lair

of your belly. Where sleeps the double sex. Walk through the
night
gently moving that thigh, that second thigh, that left leg . . .

Twenty Years A-Growing (Jeunesse)

I SUNDAY

Calculus put by, a fallen heaven I recall,
and memories sidle in to hold the house in thrall:

the old séance of rap and rhyme, of what goes on
inside the head, the spirit world, encephalon.

A horse careers off on the suburban racetrack
past ploughland, hazel groves, as if on switchback,

riddled with carbonic plague. Somewhere, who knows where,
a desperate drama queen laments her last affair —

improbable desertion. Desperadoes pine
for pandemonium and drunkenness and crime.

Along the rivers little children come and go
in straggling gangs, stifling what little curses they know.

Let us resume our studies to the rising clatter
of the workers, and the middle classes' chatter.

2 SONNET

O man of common constitution, was not the flesh
a fruit hung in the orchard? You come back in a flash,

O childhood days! Squanderable treasure of the body.
Which to love, the peril or the power of Psyche?

The earth had hillsides blossoming with men of art
and power; and lineage and race inclined your heart

to crimes and mourning — the world your fortune
and your peril. But with that labour long since proven,

you, your calculations!, are no more than your dance
and voice, unfixed, unforced, though of a double consequence,

invention and achievement in agreement — reciprocal
despite the image-empty universe — of that fraternal

and discreet humanity. Might and right
reflect that dance, that voice, only now appreciated.

3 TWENTY YEARS A-GROWING

The voices of instruction exiled . . . all gone sour,
that physical innocence lost hour after hour . . .

adagio. Ah, the infinite egoism
of adolescence, the studious optimism!

How full of flowers was the world that summer!
Airs and forms expiring, murmur on murmur . . .

a choir to temper impotence and absence in reprise!
A choir of crystal glasses, of nocturnal melodies . . .

indeed, so quickly do the nerves take up the chase
the foremost runner finds he comes last in the race.

4 WAR

Child that I was, certain skies refined my optic:
my physiognomy was changed by Zodiac.

The Phenomena were set in motion. Still —
eternally inflected Now — mathematical

infinity pursues me through the world, where I
endure the approbation of society,

respected by strange childhoods, by enormous
feelings whether troubled or harmonious.

I dream of a war of right and might, a logic
unforeseen as simple as a phrase of music.

coda

Genius (Génie)

He is affection and he is the present, since he has made the house open to the foam of winter and to the murmur of summer, he who has purified the drinks, the food — he who is the charm of fleeting places and the superhuman joy of lingering.

He is affection and he is the future, love and strength which we, upright in our rages and our boredoms, see flitting through the tempestuous sky and the ecstatic banners.

He is love: he is perfect, reinvented measure; he is marvellous and unexpected reason, and eternity: beloved instrument of fatal qualities. We have all known the terror of his concessions, and of ours; O thrill of health, the swooping upwards of our faculties, our self-considering affection and our passion for him — he who loves us for his unending life . . .

And we remember him, and he journeys . . . And if the Adoration bell resounds and goes, so does the bell of his promise: Away, superstitions, away! Those former bodies, those ménages, those ancient times, away! Ours is the era that has foundered!

He will not go away, he will not descend again from any heaven to redeem the wrath of women, nor the gaiety of men, nor all this sin. For it is done, he being and being loved.

O the surges of his breathing, head following head, his swooping off: O terrible celerity in the perfecting of forms and action.

O fecundity of mind, the immensity of the universe!

His body! The dreamed deliverance, the shattering of grace crossed by new violence!

To behold him and behold him! All the ancient genuflections and penalties revoked at his passing.

His day! The abolition of all sonorous and arbitrary sufferings, in a more plangent music.

His step! Vaster than migrations, than ancient invasions.

O him and us! Pride more compassionate than squandered charities.

O world, the glassy song of fresh disasters!

He has known us all and has loved us all: may we learn, this winter night — from tumultuous pole to castle, cape to rocky cape, from crowd to beach, from glance to gaze, our strength and feelings ebbed — to hail him, and to see him, to return him to his echo; and from under the tides and high in the wastes of snow to follow all that he beholds: the surges of his breathing, his body, and his day.

Acknowledgements

These versions are based on the French text in Rimbaud, *Illuminations*, in a new translation by Louis Varèse, New Directions, 1946, with some alternative readings from Arthur Rimbaud, *Collected Poems*, introduced and edited by Oliver Bernard, Penguin Classics, 1962.

Acknowledgement is due to the *TLS* where some of this work was published first.